AF584440

PAUL WORSLEY

A SMACK of Jellyfish

ILLUSTRATED BY HANNAH TAUFAN

REDBACK publishing

Zelly was a jellyfish
who lived all by herself.
She bobbed around the ocean
like a lonely piece of kelp.

Not knowing where her family was
or if she even had one,

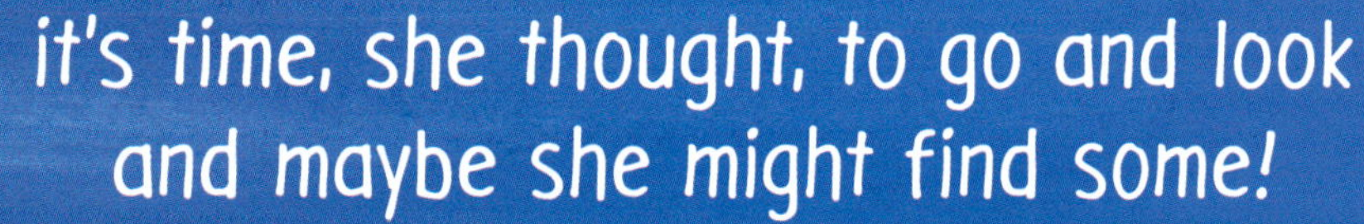

it's time, she thought, to go and look
and maybe she might find some!

The first group that she came across
were just the place to start.

'Are you my forever family?'
Zelly bravely asked.

'Sorry, Zelly, you're a jelly
and we're a **Shiver of Sharks**!'

'A Shiver of Sharks?
Well that sounds cool!'
she simply had to say.

Zelly thanked her
new-found friends
and continued on her way.

Floating through the big wide blue, she came across another.

Group of what, she's not quite sure,
could one of them be ... *Mother?*

So she decides to ask again,
'Are you my family or my friends?'

'Sorry, Zelly, you're a jelly
and we're a **Cast of Crabs**!'

'A Cast of Crabs? Incredible!'
she simply had to say.

Zelly thanked her new-found friends
and continued on her way.

On she bobbed, that jellyfish, until she found another.

Group of what, she's not quite sure,
could one of them be ... *Father?*

So she decides to ask again,
'Are you my family or my friends?'

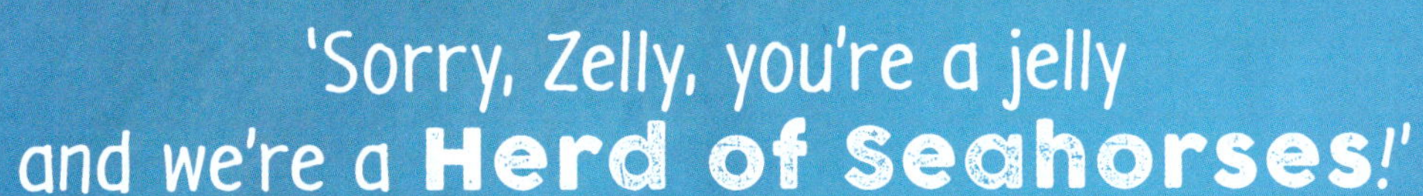

'Sorry, Zelly, you're a jelly
and we're a **Herd of Seahorses**!'

'A Herd of Seahorses? Oh, wow!'
she simply had to say.

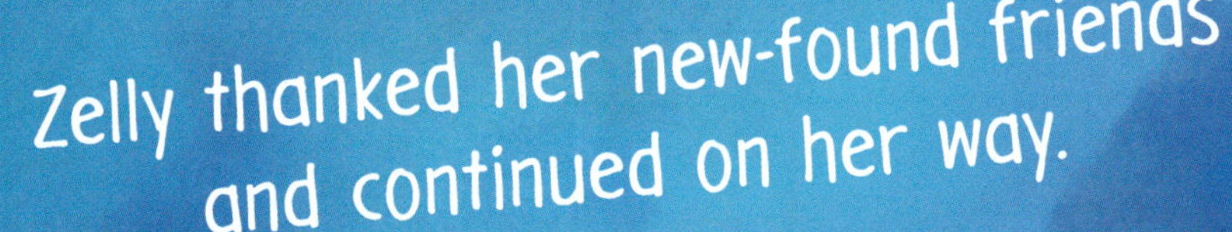

Zelly thanked her new-found friends
and continued on her way.

On she pulsed, that jellyfish, until she found another.

Group of what, she's not quite sure,
could one of them be ... *Brother?*

So she decides to ask again,
'Are you my family or my friends?'

'Sorry, Zelly, you're a jelly
and we're a **Pod of Dolphins**!'

'A Pod of Dolphins? Are you sure?'
she simply had to ask.

Zelly thanked her new-found friends
and continued with her task.

Zelly Jelly showed such courage,
never giving up.

searching through the ocean,
she just knew to **never stop**.

Until she found her family,
onwards Zelly **roamed**.

Knowing deep down in her heart
that she would find her **home**.

Drifting through the big wide blue
with no-one to assist her,
she came across another group,
could one of them be ... *Sister?*

So she decides to ask again,
'Are you my family or my friends?'

'Sorry, Zelly, you're a jelly
and we're a **Party of Rainbow Fish**!'

'A Party of Rainbow Fish? Unreal!'
she simply had to say.

Zelly thanked her new-found friends
and continued on her way.

So, on she bobbed
and on she pulsed,
searching near and far,

until she finds another group,
could one of them be ... *Pa?*

So she decides to ask again,
'Are you my family or my friends?'

'Sorry, Zelly, you're a jelly and we're a **Bale of Turtles**!'

'A Bale of Turtles? Oh how cute!'
she simply had to say.

Zelly thanked
her new-found friends
and continued
on her way.

Floating through the water
Zelly kept on meeting friends.

Which was just fine but, truth be told,
she kept on wondering, ***when?***

When might she find her family?
Are they anywhere at all?

It feels like she's just swimming
up against a great big wall.

Yet…

On she swims and on she bobs,
and spots a group that's silver.

She's not quite sure what they might be,
could one of them be ... *Grandma?*

So, Zelly bravely asks again,
'Are you my family or my friends?'

'Sorry, Zelly, you're a jelly
and we're a **Fever of Rays!**'

'A Fever of Rays? Well just no way!'
she simply had to say.

Zelly thanked her new-found friends
and continued on her way.

More determined now than ever, Zelly must stay strong

and listen to her little heart,
for how could it be wrong?

She came across a Squad of Squid
and said, 'Hi, my name's Zelly.

Have you seen a group like me?
I think I am a jelly.'

The **Squad of Squid** all stood up straight
and listened quite intently.

The leader of that Squad of Squid, she broke it to her gently.

*'We know that you've been looking all around the big wide blue,
but we have not seen any kind of jellyfish like you'.*

Drifting with the current,
Zelly hopes this is the one...

the group that is her family,
she just so wants to belong!

So Zelly bravely asks again, 'Are you my family or my friends?'

'Sorry, Zelly, you're a jelly and we're a **Family of Sardines!**'

'A Family...?' Zelly stopped.
'Of sardines!' she had to say.

Zelly sadly thanked her friends
and continued on her way.

The next group that she sees starts a stir within her heart.

'Are **you** my forever family?' Zelly bravely asks.

'YES, Zelly,
you're a jelly and we're a
smack of Jellyfish!'

'A Smack of Jellyfish?

OH, YAY!!'

Zelly screams with sheer delight.

Her new-found family hug her,
squeezing hard with all their might!

Zelly stops and finally knows
her constant search was right!

At last,
she found her family, her true **forever home**.

Here are even more fascinating collective nouns for our underwater animals:
A Pod of Whales
A Float of Tuna
A Battery of Barracudas

A Glide of Flying Fish
Can you find and name some of the other animal friends in the book?
HINT – you can find them with: 1. The Shiver of Sharks 2. The Party of Rainbow Fish 3. The Bale of Turtles 4. The Fever of Rays
A Glint of Goldfish

About the Author

Paul Worsley is an author and photographer whose life revolves around the sea. Whether it's surfing above it or swimming with the amazing creatures below, it is a lifelong love affair.

Paul graduated in 1998 and has been a professional photographer ever since. He now also dreams up stories in a little old cottage by the ocean in Sydney. This is his debut picture book.

About the Illustrator

Hannah Taufan is a youth worker and self-taught artist from Sydney's Northern Beaches. In her spare time she is often seen frantically chasing her children up the beach and searching for a surf. Her passion for art led her to a car park conversation with the author, Paul - about this magical book. You are now holding the illustrations that jumped straight from the sea and into your imagination.

For Bodhi.
The journey can be
just as beautiful as the destination.
Never give up on your search.

First Published 2025 by
Redback Publishing
Suite 6, 13a Narabang Way,
Belrose NSW 2085
Australia

www.redbackpublishing.com
email: info@redbackpublishing.com

ISBN: 978-1-761402-04-3 – HBK

Author: Paul Worsley
Illustrator: Hannah Taufan

NATIONAL LIBRARY OF AUSTRALIA
A catalogue record for this book is available from the National Library of Australia

Answers from the previous page: 1. Octopus, Coral and Conchs. **2.** Starfish, Clams and Coral. **3.** Coconut Crabs, Coral and Molluscs. **4.** Sea Snakes.